This book is to be returned on or before ... ...tional publicatio.... ...lighting the work of organisations funded by South West Arts.

South West Arts is the official public body for the arts in the South West. We cover the unitary authority areas of Bristol, Bath & North East Somerset, North Somerset, South Gloucestershire, Plymouth and Torbay, and the counties of Cornwall, Devon, Dorset (except for Bournemouth, Christchurch and Poole), Gloucestershire and Somerset.

South West Arts is one of England's ten Regional Arts Boards, receiving government funding passed to us by the Arts Council of England and from local authorities across the South West.

southwest arts

THANK YOU

My thanks go to all those who have given their time and energies to help with the creation of this publication, and particularly to the ACTA staff team: Helen Tomlin, Jane Selman, Alan May, James King, Kelly Turner, and also Lizzie Minnion, Holly Thomas, John Loosely, Marion Jones, Vania Mills, Robin Grant, Tim Atack, Rod Terry and Paul Batten, all of whom worked on the *Making a Difference* project and helped to make it such a success; to the individuals and communities who took part in *Making a Difference*; to all those who took time to complete *Turning Points* questionnaires. My thanks also go to the many professional workers and community members who played such an important role in the *Making a Difference* project: Penny McKissock, Lin Lewis, Dave Chrisfield, Betty Kiliminster, Mike McDonald, Cheryl, all the Steering Committee members for all the projects, Phil Humphries, Claire Novak and Rev. Heather Williams. My particular thanks go to the Community Fund who, as the National Lottery Charities Board, had the foresight and imagination to fund the *Making a Difference* project. My grateful thanks also to Katie Venner at South West Arts for providing the opportunity to publish *Turning Points*, and to Mary Schwarz for making sense of it all.

Neil Beddow

FOREWORD

I set out to write *Turning Points* in 1997, with the fixed idea of finding some way to prove that an individual's participation in the arts could have a beneficial effect on their participation in wider community life and indeed could, in some circumstances, have a profound influence on their future life direction. As a practitioner for nearly two decades, I have seen countless examples of people undergoing major life changes following their participation in community theatre. I see the process happening constantly: sometimes slowly, almost imperceptibly over a prolonged period; sometimes instant, dramatic.

At the time I set out to find a way of documenting and proving this case, it seemed an unpopular notion. I was sure that what I was trying to prove would be dismissed as the ravings of a crank, the over-enthusiasm of an inveterate enthusiast.

I've been very surprised to see how the climate of understanding has changed over the period from 1997 to 2001. The beneficial effect of the arts on participants is now an accepted fact.

I feel, in common with many colleagues, like a person who has been banging on a closed door for a very long time finding it suddenly flung open before them, greeted with welcoming smiles as a long-lost friend and honoured guest. The reactions of surprise and delight are mixed, perhaps understandably, with confusion and not a small degree of suspicion. It is hard to believe that no one heard the knocking before this, that the smiles are genuine, that the welcome will last.

For me, and thousands of other community artists, this is a major turning point for our sector. We have the opportunity to effect real change in the way that the arts are seen in this country. For the first time ever the work of community artists is being regarded as of national significance. The current is drawing us to the mainstream. This is what so many people have worked for, the chance to gain recognition for the arts as an integral and essential part of all people's lives, rather than a peripheral activity for an intellectual or privileged elite.

With this opportunity comes scrutiny. The claims we make for the effect of our work will be monitored, analysed and evaluated to an extent that will cause untold frustration within the community arts sector. We need to work with funding and government bodies to determine a sensitive, workable model to assess the impact of participation on individuals, and, further, on the communities in which they live.

The most compelling evidence remains the self-perception of participants themselves, the anecdotes and stories, the startling examples:

- overcoming serious lack of self-confidence to become a local councillor

- leaving drug dependency for a degree in theatre

- moving on from being a survivor in a mental health drop-in to taking the floor before hundreds of psychiatrists

The proof is in the people.

INTRODUCTION

In 1981 I was a businessman, regional manager for a firm that installed and serviced computer games in leisure facilities. Although I had always had a keen interest in the arts, and particularly in theatre, I had always felt excluded from the world of professional arts. The arts were something, I had learned to believe, that could only be created by special people, people of talent and genius, rare and strange creatures that inhabited a world of marvels. As a young man born and brought up on a council estate in the Black Country, that world seemed far removed from me. It was something I could admire, something to which I could aspire, but something that was closed to me. I had been convinced that I had nothing to offer, and so, like so many of us, didn't bother to offer it. Too scared.

Then came my turning point. Sitting in the bar of the Bristol Arts Centre after a show, I was approached by Alistair Moir, Director of Bush Telegraph Theatre in Education Company who were branching out to produce a community play, and were *"desperate for men"*. I was spun a line and got hooked. I discovered rapidly that there was another way of looking at the arts and who created them. I learned that there was creativity within all people, including myself, that was untapped, going stale and sour and making people unhappy. I found the alternative world of community arts.

'Community Arts takes as its starting
point that everyone is creative and that,
essentially, everyone is an artist.... (It)...
grew up as a response to the elitist
approach of schools and arts institutions,
which exclude the majority from being
involved in the production of art'.[1]

It is not an exaggeration to say that my
involvement in this community play changed
my life. It did: radically, extensively, nigh on
completely. The experience of working with a
wide range of different people of all ages and
classes, all discovering and using their creativity
to a common end - and, as a result, growing in
confidence and finding a sense of purpose -
shattered my preconceptions about art, creativity

---

1 Webster, Mark (ed) *Finding Voices, Making Choices*
(Nottingham: Educational Heretics Press, 1997)

and its importance to people. Within three months of the end of the play, I had left my job for that of Assistant Administrator with Bush Telegraph. I halved my salary and swapped my company car for a bike. I was just about the happiest I had ever been.

When Bush Telegraph folded due to funding cuts two years later, I went freelance as a drama facilitator and arts administrator, did a Postgraduate Certificate in Education (PGCE) in Drama, and in 1985 co-founded, with Caroline Green, Avon Community Theatre Agency (which later became ACTA Community Theatre). I have worked for the company ever since, and in 1990, when the old collective days of the 70s and 80s finally proved unworkable, became Artistic Director.

The reason for all this detail is to give my own personal dimension to the creation of this work. I am, if you like, a very clear example of the belief underlying the material, that participation in the arts has a positive and definable impact on the lives of those who participate. I am not the only one suggesting this, and certainly not the first. I can only add the weight of my experience and research to the evidence. In *Turning Points* I have tried to identify the particularities and peculiarities of the ways in which ACTA has sought to practise community theatre since 1985 and to demonstrate the effect of participation on the lives of a range of individuals from ACTA projects, in particular our *Making a Difference* project.

The roots of **community theatre** lie not only at the very beginning of the theatre form, but also at the beginning of communication.

History and national context

The ACTA Model

HISTORY AND NATIONAL CONTEXT

'Performance rooted in local communities has probably been part of life since humankind realised there was more to life than hunting and gathering.'[2]

The roots of community theatre lie not only at the very beginning of the theatre form, but also at the beginning of communication. It is likely that physical enactment of events came before language and that stories, information, emotions and opinions were passed between early peoples by gesture, mime and enactment - a form of theatre.

In this country the tradition of guild plays, mystery plays and mummers' plays were all forms where 'non-professionals' were the producers and participants. As the idea and practice of professional players and companies became the norm, the creation of theatre by ordinary people was looked down upon. In Shakespeare's *A Midsummer Night's Dream* we can detect the rot well set in, as the lords and ladies (and the professional playwright) sneer at the performance by the mechanicals. But surely in the persons of Bottom and company we have the essence of the community play. A group of people get together to make theatre, use their own ideas and creativity, design and make their own sets and costumes, adapt the script to their

---

2 'Community Plays', *MAILOUT* (February/March 1999)

own devices and work together to cast and produce the show. There is even, in Peter Quince, a facilitator for the group: patient, encouraging, accommodating, his sole aim to *'entreat, request and desire'* his companions to learn their parts.

Amateur theatre has a long tradition in this country, matched by an equally long tradition of the term 'amateur' being one of derision and censure. The historical pageant and its re-emergence in the twentieth century has been pointed to as a root of the community play, as has the work of the Unity Players[3] groups that sprang up in the 1930s. There is also evidence of some large-scale proto-community play projects in the 1960s, growing from the development of community theatre companies. The re-emergence of the community play in the last thirty years has its roots in the work of Peter Cheeseman at the Victoria Theatre in Stoke on Trent, the documentary plays of the Living Archive in Milton Keynes, and particularly in the work of Ann Jellico and the Colway Theatre Trust, established in 1979. By 1981 there were community plays happening in different parts of the country, including the one in Bristol that began my career in the arts.

Since then there has been a remarkable proliferation of the form, with many communities, villages, towns and cities across Britain creating community plays. The phenomenon has involved many people in the arts for the first time, and has proved to be a successful and regularly used vehicle for the promotion of civic pride.

3 These developed from workers' amateur dramatics clubs: an example is the Bristol Unity Players Club formed by Joan Tuckett in 1936.

Many communities have chosen the community play to celebrate the Millennium. In this country a national body has been formed to advocate the work, Community Plays UK[4], and the community play movement has spread to different parts of the world, notably North America and Australia.

The community play of modern times has been defined succinctly by Richard Hayhow of the Open Theatre Company[5] in nine points:

1. a large cast in the region of 100 people

2. a role for any member of the community who wants to be involved

3. participation in all areas of the process

4. a core professional team, including writer and director

5. a long set-up period (up to two years)

6. a play specially written and adapted for the community and expressing its wishes, needs and concerns, often a celebratory event

7. an innovative performance style including a role for the audience in the performance

8. a variety of community activities happening alongside it and related to it

9. a commitment to develop future activities after the play

---

4 The Theatre Museum houses the full National Community Plays Archive and Database; the C-PAD database can be accessed through the Open Theatre Company website as below.

5 http://www.opentheatre.co.uk

This is only one definition, and there are elements with which many companies and practitioners would take issue, but it serves as a starting point.

David Jones[6] sets out two models as defined by the practice of the Colway Theatre Trust and the work of the Belgrade Theatre in Coventry:

In the **Colway Model**, work:	In the **Belgrade Model**, work:
is written	is devised
is in the mainstream theatre tradition	is in the community arts tradition
is largely historical	is largely issue-based
is product-focused	is process-focused
uses participation	explores collaboration
can be termed community theatre	can be termed communal theatre

David Jones classifies ACTA's work as a 'hybrid form' of the above. It is more a case of parallel evolution. ACTA's work, policy, code of practice and constituencies are all influences on how our model developed. Perhaps it is better to view ACTA's work as a genus on its own.

6 Jones, D. *Aesthetic Justice and Communal Theatre: a new conceptual approach to the community play as an aspect of theatre for empowerment'* (PhD thesis University of Warwick, 1996)

THE ACTA MODEL

To borrow from David Jones' structuring above, the ACTA community play model:

1 is primarily concerned with **individual and community development**

2 determines theme and content through **community consultation**

3 is **devised then scripted**; casting takes place without auditions

4 is based on **living memory and present issues**

5 holds **process and product** as equally important, and mutually dependent

6 actively promotes **access and inclusivity** to excluded sections of community, which impacts on production style

7 has a three year **structure** - pilot projects, play, consolidation - which works towards long-term **sustainability** of projects

1 Individual and community development

'There is no good reason for the public sector to disregard the community development benefits of participation in the arts. It is in the act of creativity that empowerment lies and through sharing creativity that understanding and social inclusiveness are promoted.'[7]

ACTA's work is specifically aimed at promoting individual and community development through the medium of theatre-related arts projects. In our work, the play is not just a product but also the means to an end - creating a stronger community, building capacity, promoting the achievements of marginalised groups, redefining a community's sense of itself.

Our community play work is designed to empower individuals and their communities through:

- creating opportunities for exploring creativity
- validating individual experiences, and the history of the area
- giving a voice and a platform for expression
- creating a single focus for the energies of many
- creating an opportunity for all sections of the community to work together co-operatively

7 Matarrasso, F. *Use or Ornament? The Social Impact of Participation in the Arts* (Stroud: Comedia, 1997)

- discovering a shared identity and a reason for pride
- celebrating the unique culture of the area
- most importantly, in the whole process, fostering the development of self-confidence and self-worth, both in individuals and within the whole community

2 Community consultation

The content of a project is determined during a long process of consultation and discussion with all sections of the community in order to identify fully the issues of concern in that area. This usually results in the plays being set largely within living memory, and especially having links to, and scenes set in, the present day.

We believe that it is important to establish the ownership of the play at the very beginning of the project and to ensure that the content is seen as relevant to members of that community. This process takes time, usually beginning even before the project officially starts and continuing throughout the first year of the project, as contacts are made, pilot projects initiated and individuals involved. Throughout the devising period there is still the opportunity for the community to determine and shape the content of the play. This process ensures that the project is:

- publicised to a wide constituency
- engaging local imagination

- enfranchising the local community
- owned by local people from the beginning

If this is carried out diligently and successfully, there is a high probability that the finished play will truly reflect the community, and will 'ring true' with the members of that community.

"Loved it, brill, magic and sad because it's so true."
Audience member, *Hot Water*

3 Devised then scripted

Plays are created by local participants during a long process of discussion, improvisation, play-making and writing. The writer acts as facilitator, enabling participants to use their creativity to interpret the material gained from the consultation process above. The play in its final state is the product of many creative minds in which people can recognise their own contribution.

"The most enjoyable thing was seeing the progress of the finished story from vague ideas to the strong final tale."
Participant, *Out of the Shadows*

We use a number of different strategies to devise a community play. Typically, a youth theatre is established in the area during the first year to work on material for the community play during year two. At the same time, a devising group, which tends to be a microcosm of the community, meets weekly throughout the project. This usually has a smallish core group of between 10 and 15, although many other people drift in and out of the process. During the course of a play's creation, including the youth theatre and involvement of other groups such as schools and day centres, up to 100 people contribute creatively to the script. The more often people attend devising sessions, the more they contribute, and the facilitator has to ensure that sessions are not taken over by a vocal few.

Devising techniques and practices vary depending on factors such as the:

- particular style of the facilitator
- physical surroundings (e.g. large groups in small rooms can't work in small groups)
- interests of the individuals in the group
- needs of the play

Some plays are almost totally created through dramatic improvisation. Participants adopt characters and create scenes spontaneously which are recorded on video or noted down by the writer/facilitator scribbling madly (e.g. *Ticket to Nowhere*). Other plays have been written 'in the circle', with a whole group slowly piecing together scenes through a collaborative effort, throwing in lines, bouncing ideas off each other (e.g. *Out of the Shadows*). Most groups, however, use a mix of different techniques, with drama and creative writing sitting comfortably side by side in the same session.

The process can often be little more than a discussion, particularly in areas where the arts are viewed with suspicion or where group members have little confidence in their contributions. In this sort of situation, the facilitator finds ways of drawing out creativity, almost without the participants noticing. During *Making a Difference*, I was accompanied to an early devising session on the Bournville estate by a student from a community arts course. The group was small, reluctant and feeling low; the prospect of tea and biscuits was more attractive than the idea of making a scene and the idea of creating a whole play seemed to them at that point insurmountable. I mentally tore up my session plan, fetched biscuits, and we chatted, vaguely and generally, about the scene we were meant to be writing and the characters in it.

When the formal task had been removed, the group was full of ideas. *"Well, she might say this..."* and *"What about if he came back?"* and *"Of course, she would think that because..."* I listened, asked the odd question, and scribbled. At the end of the two hour session, the group read together the scene we'd written that morning, with another cup of tea and a quiet sense of satisfaction. Later, the student said, *"They wrote that scene, and they didn't even know they were doing it. It just happened."*

Sometimes that's the best way of doing it. In many situations a formal plan, with a warm-up and 'arty' exercises, rather than stimulating involvement, can actually present a huge barrier to creativity. The important thing is to find what's right for that particular group on that particular day, and not to be afraid to throw away the plan and improvise.

The play is produced in collaboration between all participants, but it is the role of the writer/facilitator to take all the contributions and use them and new material to construct a play that will:

- fairly balance all contributing voices
- truly reflect the issues concerning the community
- make sense
- entertain an audience
- create enough equally-sized and suitable parts to suit the size and make-up of cast

The play has to be long enough to incorporate all the issues the devising group want to include, but not too long for an audience to appreciate. I usually encourage devising groups to aim for a first half of 1 hour 20 minutes, and a second half of 1 hour. Any more than this and the audience's experience can start to become less than comfortable; their attention will wander and the effect of the play will be less. The writing group and facilitator have to decide what to leave out, as well as what to leave in.

Balancing all this is not an easy task. No matter how much the community has been involved in the process, it's always possible that the finished play isn't quite right. To avoid this, the writer/facilitator always produces a first draft for the devising group and the steering committee of the whole project, to be agreed or changed. This is usually a simple process; in most circumstances people have been involved enough through the play-making to have ironed out any difficulties along the way. Although changes are always made, the final draft is usually fairly close to the first.

The process, however, can lend itself to abuse. One community play script, although thoroughly devised, was sent back for radical changes three times because two members of the devising group could not make up their minds about certain details. Even after three re-writings, when the final script had been accepted, the two members continued to change their minds, resulting in extensive re-writing during the rehearsal process and even during the run of the show. I think the show as performed on the last night did finally have some form of grudging approval. Whilst it is important to try to serve the desires and creativity of all members of the group, sometimes individuals may have personal reasons for disrupting the process and going against the will of the larger group.

For many people exercising their creativity for the first time in many years, devising is a revelation - particularly the experience of creating as part of a group.

"If you'd said go off and write this on my own, I couldn't have done it. But working with a partner, we had a laugh, and bounced ideas off each other, and helped each other out, and it was easy."

Jackie, Bournville devising group

The devising group feels a great sense of ownership of the play. When the script is produced, typed up from the previous week's session, the reaction of participants to seeing their work in print is one of complete delight. It's a tremendously empowering moment. This sense of pride and satisfaction is particularly evident on Script Pick-up Night.

This event is held at the very beginning of the rehearsal process. Everyone who has asked to be included in the cast is given a part, then invited to come along on a certain night to pick up their scripts, talk to the directors and staff and get a feeling for the whole play. This event has replaced the Play Read-through, when we used to get the whole cast together to read through the play. This was dropped as it created difficulties for people who found it hard to read or to concentrate for a long period of time. In other community play models, particularly the Colway model, it has been the tradition for the playwright to read through the play to the cast. ACTA have never done this, as it identifies the play too much in the ownership of the writer and doesn't recognise the community's contribution.

The casting of a play is a point of contention in many community plays. Although most community plays have a policy of casting everyone who wants a part, it doesn't mean to say that everyone gets the part they want. In the end, the play is written, and the cast must be found to fit the parts.

This is very different in ACTA's model. Our approach relates directly to our policy for devising and inclusivity. The play is written to fit the participants, rather than the participants found to fit the play. There are several reasons for this:

- **practical:** there's no point writing a play with lots of male parts if 80% of participants are women.

- **creative:** people can create the parts they want to play.

- **equality of opportunity:** every character has lines (unless they don't want them): there are no 'star parts'. There is no point in a community play that is only really about the relationship between two people.

- **inclusivity:** parts can be created for the whole range of age and abilities who want to get involved. Just because someone has no speech, or is five, or is disabled, or has a learning difficulty, or is 95, does not mean they cannot have a significant role.

There are no auditions for an ACTA show: anyone who wants to be in the play is involved. To some extent, people who are part of the devising process have the opportunity to create the role they then go on to play, so casting is an organic process. Other participants are contacted and involved as the process continues, so it's possible to ensure the final script contains enough speaking roles to reflect this. Some people become involved once the script is finished. We meet these people for a chat to discuss the sort of part they would like and incorporate this.

Participants with low literacy are given support and a taped reading of the play is made available for visually impaired participants or non-readers. Parts can be created to cater specifically for the special abilities of participants who would not be able to take part in conventional plays. One disabled participant in an ACTA show, unable to communicate except by an alphabet board, created a fully developed character and gave a greatly moving performance using facial expression and gesture that was central to the play. It is extremely important that inclusivity is not interpreted as tokenism, where (particularly) disabled people are included in the cast of a community play which is designed with no thoughts about their access needs. I have seen examples of this in shows by other companies, where wheelchair users have been part of a promenade performance that has meant that they cannot see or be seen. One stunningly insensitive production had a wheelchair user in the cast, but the raked stage made access totally impossible. The cast member was left to spend the whole show stuck at the front, desperately trying to be part of the action, until eventually, when their frustrations became apparent, they were wheeled off-stage by an embarrassed stagehand.

Living memory and present issues

As the theme and content of ACTA's community plays are based on a process of consultation and devising with community members, a large part of the subject matter comes from the personal experiences of those consulted. This is not exclusive to ACTA's work: for instance, the Belgrade Theatre, Remould Theatre in Hull and the Living Archive have included elements of oral history and documentary in their plays and often deal with present-day issues.

In our work, the present day and the past are usually linked by a narrative structure which puts the two periods in some form of context, making connections between the different life experiences, re-discovering and validating the past and its importance to the issues of the present.

In each of the estates involved in the *Making a Difference* project, there was a similarity in the basic response to the suggestion of doing a play based on the history of the area, summarised as:

"It'll be a short play then. There's nothing to do a play about. Nothing's ever happened round here."

It required a great leap of faith for people to recognise that they had a past at all, let alone one to be celebrated, one of which to be proud. Yet, once the reminiscence started, once interviewees were aware that, yes, we did want to know about the minute details of their history, and yes, we did find it fascinating, they also became aware of the importance of their own experiences, and the particular significance of their own existence. We all have a story to tell: what we normally lack is someone to whom to tell it. It is easy within our internal worlds to become convinced of our own unimportance, our lack of influence upon events.

"I've been waiting 40 years to tell this story, and this is the first time anyone really wanted to listen."

Ralph, Bournville estate

The interest that the community play project showed in individual experiences led the interviewees to look again at and re-assess their experiences. If someone else was interested in their life, then their life was interesting. If someone else valued their life, then their life was valuable. Validated. When that story is turned into theatre, seen by an audience who are interested in, entertained and moved by the stories and details of that life, then the effect on the individual is multiplied.

Making a Difference looked for stories around which to build each play, so that the plays themselves would reflect accurately not only the individual participants, but also the history and spirit of the whole area. For an area usually regarded as a problem, a dumping ground or a hotbed of crime, a public platform is a unique opportunity to put forward a positive message, challenge prejudice and validate the experience and existence of that community.

5 Process and product

The theatre product is the means to an end, not an end in itself. The ultimate aim is the empowerment of each individual, and the community as a whole, through a process of self-discovery. Stressing the importance of participation in this process, however, does not mean that the product is unimportant. It is of the greatest importance. It is the sum total of the effort, creativity and energy of all those involved. All members of the project have a stake in it and a share in its outcome. If it fails, then their share is failure; if it succeeds, their share is success. It is therefore imperative that the show is of the highest possible quality in relation to the:

- aspirations of the participants
- expectations of the audience
- overall aims of the project
- needs of the area

The measures of success can vary from project to project, but usually have core elements:

- size of audience
- press coverage
- enjoyment of audience
- atmosphere of project - if it's too tense, there's no fun
- it happening at all
- the message getting across
- spin-offs post play
- artistic quality of finished product

6 Access and inclusivity

Most community play projects are open to all-comers, but ACTA's projects try to be open to non-comers too – those who exclaim, *"Oh no, not me!"*. It's not enough to have an 'open door'; after all, a door, open or not, suggests that you are inviting people into your world, a world which they have to enter. To people used to being excluded, an open door is in a sense still closed. To people used to being rejected, 'everyone welcome' will still not include them. It will mean, everyone with experience, everyone with talent, everyone who can read the poster, everyone who can walk up the steps to the rehearsal room, everyone who is important, everyone who matters'. Everyone except themselves.

Communities often in most need of the re-invigorating and empowering qualities of community arts are often those most unlikely to put themselves forward - the 'socially excluded' in the latest definition. ACTA interprets this as those on low incomes, people with a disability (including people with learning difficulties and people with mental health needs), older people, people living in areas with poor facilities, single parent families. We target these sections of the community for inclusion in community play projects with a programme of outreach sessions, visits and informal conversations, using the networks of statutory and voluntary organisations in each community. Often we design pilot projects to involve these groups and individuals in familiar and comfortable settings to build confidence and relationships before embarking on the larger project.

Typical projects have included reminiscence theatre which link young people with older people from sheltered accommodation. Elders relate memories to young people who use them as material for dramatic improvisation, creating short plays that are presented back to elders. We also work closely with local authority day centres to set up pilot projects with people with learning difficulties, enabling them to become members of the cast or crew of the community play. In some areas we set up out-of-school theatre groups to involve children and young people in small-scale projects which develop their skills, confidence and commitment prior to the main project.

Pilot projects like this result in a much wider community representation in the community play. The benefits of this process are significant, not only for the development of those individuals' confidence and friendship networks, but for the wider community, where people find themselves working closely with others with whom, in normal circumstances, they would have no contact.

It is essential that any space used during a project - for a meeting, rehearsal or performance - is fully accessible. Most of ACTA's shows are played on the floor with the audience raised around it, either in the round, traverse or arena style. People using wheelchairs or with reduced mobility then have no physical obstacle to their taking part. Shows are never performed in theatres, which are notoriously inaccessible, but in school halls, community centres and industrial spaces, where it is possible to create accessible performance spaces.

This focus on inclusivity impacts also on choice of production style. ACTA rarely uses the promenade style that some other companies favour, where the action is on several stages between which the audience moves. We find this form places the audience under duress. It is tiring for just about anyone to stand for two and a half hours. For many members of the audience - children, some older people, wheelchair users and smaller people - the view is limited, the atmosphere claustrophobic and the experience wholly frustrating.

7 Structure and sustainability

The community play projects initiated by ACTA have a basic structure, usually stretching over a three-year period:

Pre-project

- Contact made between community and ACTA
- Agreement to work in partnership
- Research into basic issues concerning area
- Steering committee formed
- Project plan drawn up by ACTA in partnership with steering committee
- Funding sought
- Research into stakeholders and potential partner organisations

Phase one

(once funding found)

- Co-ordinator in post
- Research into local issues, contact with local groups
- Meetings - public and targeted to specific organisations and groups
- Pilot projects - small-scale participatory arts projects aimed at socially excluded groups
- Consultation process to determine issues, content and theme for play
- Devising groups begin to meet

Phase two

- Devising group continues to develop script through improvisation, playmaking and writing
- Process extended to other community groups e.g. schools, targeted groups
- Participants from community engaged in process of playmaking
- Script completed
- Show rehearsed, set built, costumes made, music written
- Show performed
- After show meeting to determine future

Phase three

– Co-ordinator continues

– Steering committee develops its role

– Follow-on projects agreed at end of year two
  are established

– Second large-scale project (if identified as a
  follow-on project)

– Smaller-scale community arts projects
  (if identified as follow-on projects)

– Preparation of the steering committee to
  manage on-going projects (if wished)

ACTA's projects aim to create
and maintain sustainable
organisations that can continue
after the end of the initial
project. *Making a Difference*
was set up to explore further
the ways to do this.

ACTA applied for and were successful in obtaining funding for the three year development project *Making a Difference*, which ran from April 1996 to March 1999

Project aims
Area profiles
Making it work

MAKING A DIFFERENCE

In 1995, ACTA were at a turning point in its development. At its inception a decade earlier the company had set out a clear policy for its work in community theatre that had led to a wide range of projects. This included the establishment of a youth theatre and children's theatre network; projects with people with a disability and with young people at risk; two festivals of theatre by people with learning difficulties; issue-based work with young people; and a commitment to the development of community plays.

Two of these community plays were particularly important to us: the Southmead Community Play *Lifelines* in 1994 and the South Bath Community Play *The South Side Sisters* in 1995. Both were based on council estates with high poverty indicators and negative images in the wider community, with little, if any, experience of community arts projects and no experience of community theatre. In both areas the projects had a huge impact on individuals and the communities within which they lived. However funding was a problem.

ACTA had several points to consider, including the:

- success of its community play model, particularly in disadvantaged areas
- subsequent need to fulfil demands from communities to sustain projects in these areas

- demands from other communities for community play work
- difficulties of raising funds for community play projects - due mostly to the lack of understanding by funding bodies about the benefits of the work, and a lack of evidence about its impact

Here was a huge opportunity for the company to draw together the threads of its community play work into one project, a project which targeted this work into disadvantaged areas, and which had at its core the community play model we had created over the previous ten years. Experience had shown that this model, although it had its faults, worked, and that participation in ACTA projects had shown a high rate of positive change in individuals and communities.

The opportunity existed; the demand was there. The probability of success was high, and, with the creation of the National Lotteries Charities Board (NLCB), there was the possibility of funding under their Poverty and Disadvantage programme. ACTA applied for and were successful in obtaining funding for the three year development project *Making a Difference*, which ran from April 1996 to March 1999.

PROJECT AIMS

Making a Difference used theatre as a medium for individual and community development in four council estates in the South West, all of which were areas of high social stress. Our aims were:

- to work in partnership with local residents of all ages, particularly those who did not normally get involved in community activities: single parents and their children, older people, people with learning difficulties, unemployed people

- to create work that:
  - addressed local issues
  - fostered a sense of community spirit by providing a voice for local concerns
  - provided a focus for discussion
  - drew wide attention to the positive aspects and potential of people in the estates
  - challenged the negative stereotypes that contribute to a sense of disempowerment
  - developed skills to enable full independence from ACTA

We set the following measures of achievement for each area:

- a performance based on local issues devised and created by local people, staged at a local venue to an audience of at least 1000

- evidence of growth in self-esteem, confidence and ability to articulate views and opinions

- trained individuals who had shadowed professionals in fundraising, artistic direction, theatre administration, design, sound, and lighting
- a one-year skills training course
- 150 - 200 people involved in each year of the project
- an independent community theatre group, run by and for local people, to be in place at the end of three years, capable of taking decisions about how they wished to develop their theatre resource

Collection of this evidence was through a process of monitoring and evaluation built into the project. The methodology included participant feedback forms; audience questionnaires; photographic record; professional community worker feedback; community meetings.

Our basic project plan for the three years accommodated the different levels and types of activity that had already happened in each of the areas: Southmead, South Bath, Stoke Gifford, Bournville. This meant, for instance, that *Making a Difference* took place in Southmead only for the first year, but for all three years in Bournville.

AREA PROFILES

1 Southmead

Southmead ward is a recognisable neighbourhood with 12,000 residents and 4,000 households. There are two small neighbourhood retail areas including a newly-opened low-cost supermarket. A high proportion of retail properties are empty, many have been vandalised over the years; there is no bank or building society. The area has a day nursery, four primary schools and a secondary school. Purpose-built leisure facilities for young people are limited and open public spaces have suffered from neglect and a lack of investment. Early death rates are high and the area has the highest incidence of possession of drugs in Bristol.

- **45%** of housing is local authority owned
- **6.6%** of working age residents overall are unemployed (Bristol average 5.7%) of which 14.3% are long-term unemployed and 30% young people
- **25%** of residents are under 16
- **34%** of households have dependent children[8]

8 Statistics for area profiles from *Bristol Crime and Disorder Audit* (Bristol: Bristol Community Safety Partners, 1999) and Office of Population Censuses and Surveys *1991 Census* (London: HMSO, 1992)

2 South Bath

The five estates covered by *Making a Difference* - Southdown, Whiteway, Odd Down, Oldfield Park, Twerton - are geographically adjacent, situated to the south of Bath. Residents in the area have poorer than average health, with a high incidence of heart disease. There is a recognised drugs problem, especially among young people, and a connected high crime rate, particularly in Whiteway.

- **28%** of housing is local authority owned in the area overall, with higher percentages in Whiteway, Odd Down, Southdown and Twerton (the latter being almost 50%)
- **8.9%** of working age residents are unemployed
- **51%** of households are without a car

3 The Stokes

The Stokes covers a section of North Bristol and the south of South Gloucestershire - Patchway, Filton, Little Stoke, Stoke Gifford, Bradley Stoke and Harry Stoke. This is an isolated area on the outskirts of Bristol with poor public transport, few facilities and a high percentage of ex-mental hospital patients living in the community. Stoke Gifford is a parish of approximately 5000 households bisected by a main road. The ward of Stoke Gifford North comprises Little Stoke, a former farming region where fields were first built upon to house railway workers, with greater development taking place from the 1950s due to the aerospace industries. Most of the population lives in social housing and there is a high percentage of single parent families and people on low incomes. The old village of Stoke Gifford in the ward of Stoke Gifford South was not developed to such an extent until later; a higher percentage of the property is owner-occupied.

- **28%** of housing is local authority/housing association owned
- **8%** of working age residents are unemployed
- **4%** of households are lone-parent families
- **20%** of residents are aged over 65

4 Bournville

The Bournville estate, population 5,500, is situated to the south of Weston-Super-Mare in North Somerset. It has the highest level of poverty in the whole of the county, receives Single Regeneration Budget funding and is a designated Education Action Zone. There is a recognised drugs problem in the area and higher than the county average figures for infant deaths, smoking, alcohol abuse, obesity, long-term illness, heart disease, lung cancer and premature death.

- **66%** of housing is local authority owned
- **34%** of working age residents are unemployed (county average 6.8%)
- **29.2%** of households are single parent families
- **35%** of under 21s have children under 5 (county average 15%)
- **52%** of households are without a car

MAKING IT WORK

1 Southmead

When *Making a Difference* started, the
Southmead project had been in existence for
three years. It had already been through the
phases of initial contact, steering committee,
devising, production of first community play,
second production, and the members of the
steering committee had gained a great deal of
confidence in their aspirations for creating
community theatre in the area. So our aim here
during the first year of *Making a Difference* was
to provide training programmes in a range of
theatre-related skills as would usually happen in
the third year of the ACTA community play project
model. Steering committee members had formed
an independent arts organisation, CATS
(Community Action Theatre Southmead), and
were running youth theatre sessions that were
led by three members of the steering committee,
all women over 60. Unfortunately the sessions
were plagued by problems including:
inexperience of the leaders in planning sessions
and dealing with youth issues; the make-up of the
group - some with experience through the
community plays, others new to theatre; the
venue; disagreements between young people and
disagreements between the leaders of the group.

In *Making a Difference* we wanted to provide
more formal training opportunities than in
previous projects and, responding to the
situation, began a series of weekly workshops in

association with CATS in September 1996. We aimed to provide training in specific skill areas identified by CATS - writing, devising, drama workshop skills, directing, lighting and design - to enhance their youth theatre sessions. Attendance was very good, with over 20 people coming each week, but the sessions never quite achieved what they set out to. Although the group attracted many experienced adults and young people who had been involved in the other projects, about half of the group were young people with no previous experience. Many of them had to bring their younger brothers and sisters: all free activities were seen as opportunities for childcare. It was also a cold and wet autumn, attracting some young people with no interest in developing theatre skills, only in finding warmth and shelter.

This led to tension between the expectations and needs of the different participants that could not be resolved in one common session. Various attempts were made to sort out the problems: the session was extended and split into two, with drama training sessions first, for more experienced members, and a youth theatre second, for beginners. This in turn led to tension with the three women leading the CATS youth theatre who felt that this would clash with their own sessions, and so ended after a few weeks.

The venue was problematical too. The original meeting place was a church hall with no security and our move to a large community centre with door staff, to prevent disruption from those just seeking shelter, led to further problems. This new space was in a different part of the estate from where most group members lived; it was a little too far to walk to on a dark night through someone else's territory. The rehearsal space was a small room on the top floor of a large complex where lots of other activities were going on. The noisy devising of the group disturbed other users, which led to some difficulties between centre staff and some of the teenage members of the group.

The CATS group, with our support, decided to devise and stage a youth theatre show as a means of providing a platform for the group to re-launch itself and gain new members. The group met during the spring of 1997 and ACTA workers facilitated sessions with the members, creating a structure, some songs and a range of sketches for a show to be called *'Young (at heart) and living in Southmead'*. Although much progress was made with the group, it was difficult trying to arrange a time and a place for the show.

The committee that managed CATS ran into many internal difficulties, caused in the main by a clash of personalities. It had reached the stage where meetings could not happen without a community worker or mediation officer present. ACTA tried on three occasions to work with the group to plan for the future, aware that the funding for this third and last year of development was rapidly running out. However, agreements reached at one meeting were refuted at the next, and it proved impossible to proceed.

Southmead factfile

- 40 young people and 10 adults involved in workshops
- 40 sessions facilitated
- a youth theatre created and led by local people
- a six-month informal training scheme
- more interest in the arts on the estate
- involvement in an Arts Forum project for the area
- participants in the project took a major part in community development and regeneration initiatives in the area
- plans made for a long-term youth theatre project

Although the project did not produce the self-sustaining group planned at the outset of *Making a Difference*, it still had an impact on the area and in particular on many of the individuals who took part.

"I gained enormous self-esteem from the project: it was a highlight in my life. We still enjoy watching the video and chatting about the play."

Pauline Bryant, Southmead

One woman with a disability is now a performance poet and many of the young people have developed interests in drama and dance. Calls for a youth theatre for the area came from a group of young people who were involved throughout the project and who are now of an age to take a positive role in facilitation and management.

2 | **South Bath**

ACTA had been working in the South Bath area for two years prior to the start of *Hot Water*, the first *Making a Difference* project here, and had been instrumental in working with local people to set up SWOOT Community Theatre. From July 1994 to July 1995 over 100 people from the south side of Bath took part in the creation and performance of a large-scale community play, *The South Side Sisters*. This project was such a success - artistically, in terms of community development and educationally - that people involved in the project decided to develop another play. The success of the skills training course which ran alongside the first project ensured the support of Bath and North East Somerset Community Education which then funded a series of workshops in devising, scripting and play-making. There were some 'taster' sessions in the autumn of 1995, and the project started in earnest in January 1996, continuing with the benefit of the NLCB funding.

Hot Water

Over 30 people from SWOOT Community Theatre who had been involved in *The South Side Sisters* gathered for preliminary devising sessions. The group varied in ages from teenagers to older people and included people with learning difficulties and disabled people. At these sessions people were involved in brainstorming, small group work and whole group discussion to determine the possible theme and content for the next show. After several sessions, the group decided to concentrate on the theme of money and the two Baths. A simple but remarkably creative plot was devised, involving the diversion of the hot springs that feed the Roman Baths in the city centre to a street on a council estate on the outskirts.

A group of 20-25 people were then involved in devising and writing sessions, running both in the daytime and in evenings to allow the greatest possible access for community members. Sessions involved participants in a variety of activities geared towards inspiring and channelling their creativity: drama and improvisation; writing 'around the circle' as a whole group; writing in small groups; brainstorming; song writing; pastiche; character-building; dialogue writing. Some group members took scenes away to complete at home. I acted throughout as a central point for all the material created and was responsible for shaping and structuring it into the final script.

This process continued until July 1996, with members of the devising group editing and adapting several drafts of the play before the script of the play was finalised and sent for printing. Most members of the devising group also took part in the play and were able to play characters they had created for themselves. *"I wrote that line!"* was a commonly heard cry during the rehearsal period.

There were some difficulties at this time. The gap between the end of *The South Side Sisters* and the start of the devising session for the new show (due to lack of funding) meant that some of the participants in *The South Side Sisters* did not carry through into *Hot Water*. During the devising period in particular, it was difficult for local professional workers, with a huge workload of their own, to give the same generous degree of support they had given to the first show. Alternating each week between daytime and evening sessions led to confusion about when sessions were being held and may well have discouraged attendance. However, a smaller group of 14 people were constant members and met weekly.

The rehearsal period began in the first week in September 1996 with a Script Pick-up and Meet the Director evening. As by now I was heavily involved in the devising phase of the project in Stoke Gifford, Lizzie Minnion, ACTA's newly appointed Community Theatre Facilitator, took the role as Director and saw *Hot Water* through from script to performance in 12 weeks.

Although it had a smaller cast than *The South Side Sisters*, this second project still succeeded in meeting SWOOT Community Theatre's aim of involving all sections of the community. Participants included older people, young people, disabled people, people with learning difficulties and single mothers. There was a large number of new members and also a number of individuals who wanted to take a greater role in *Hot Water*. For instance, people who had helped to sell refreshments for the first show became important members of the cast in the second.

Carrswood Resource and Activities Centre and Whiteway Youth Club were used for rehearsals, with different cast groupings meeting on different nights to rehearse. Although Whiteway was a good rehearsal venue in terms of being accessible to young people, it proved problematic in that there was only one space, and smaller group work was therefore almost impossible. There were also many distractions to deal with from young people not involved in the project.

A team of three drama workers was assembled to lead the direction, with one participant from the local community assuming the role of Assistant Director, learning appropriate skills by shadowing the Director.

During the production period ACTA led a series of design courses for local people in set, costume and lighting skills. The set included an outstanding 40 foot square floorcloth, painted in Roman mosaic, and an on-stage hot spring, complete with real water! Participants used their new skills to design, rig and operate the lights and also produce the sound for the show. The show also used slide and video projections - an idea generated by people on the design course. Song music was written by our musical director, Robin Grant, but was arranged and performed by a young person from the area, who was also responsible for writing and arranging incidental music.

Using a school hall as the venue for *Hot Water* had some obvious advantages over the old depot site used for *The South Side Sisters* the year before. We did not need to spend a lot of time converting the venue into a theatre and worrying about security, but could concentrate on the show itself. There were some disadvantages: the hall was used for school meals, so we had to remove the set and seating after each performance.

There were only four performances of the final show, due to limitations of time and space at the venue, and the audience wasn't that large, although good publicity had been distributed widely. We had some excellent coverage on BBC television and radio and in the press, but many people felt that the location of the venue in Oldfield Park put off a large potential audience from the Whiteway/Twerton area, from where the majority of participants came.

Here's a summary of participants' responses to the evaluation questionnaire circulated on the last day of the production.

Involvement

- **70%** were cast members; **20%** were technical; **10%** other
- **50%** had not been in *The South Side Sisters*
- **60%** came through previous experience of ACTA projects; **25%** through word of mouth; **15%** from newspapers and posters

Ratings

On a scale of 1 - 6, between poor and excellent,

- **60%** rated rehearsals between 4 - 6
- **70%** rated performance week as 5 & 6
- **90%** rated ACTA's back-up as 5 & 6

Most enjoyable

- making new friends
- the feeling of community
- the excitement of putting on the play

"My life has been richer. I have gained skills in working with people, and gained friends."

"All you lovely people and so much truth and straightness."

"People from all walks of life getting together, working together and achieving something."

Least enjoyable
(only 50% of respondents commented)

- rehearsal problems
- difficulties with the rehearsal space
- some tension between adults and children in the cast

Personal gain

- **45%** said making new friends and meeting people
- **25%** said increased confidence and skills
- **20%** mentioned community spirit and teamwork

"I have gained a real sense of community spirit, and so many new friends."

"Increased electrical knowledge and improved design skills."

"I have gained LOADS, I cannot begin to put it into words."

Hot Water factfile

- 4 performances at Hayesfield School, Bath in November 1996
- 600 in audience
- 85 in cast, 25 backstage/technical
- 25 involved in devising/scripting: 19 women, including some teenagers; 19 people with a disability including people with learning difficulties; 3 black people
- 20 involved in design workshops

Many of the participants, although registering their enjoyment and appreciation of the project, felt that after two community plays in two years they wanted to have a rest. There was also a sense of empowerment having gone as far as it could in this form. Several key members of the group, who were central to the community taking further control of SWOOT Community Theatre, moved on to employment or left the area.

In the second year of *Making a Difference*, we organised a six-week skills course in devising and writing beginning in May 1997. Even though the sessions were widely publicised, including a mail-out to all former members, attendance was disappointing. Reasons were various: the light evenings, the period of time since the last meeting, the situation of the venue. After several weeks, although ideas were flowing around the creation of a new show, the group decided to re-launch the sessions in the autumn when they felt there would be more interest.

The devising and writing sessions began again in October 1997, based at Odd Down Youth Club, with around ten group members attending on a regular basis over a ten-week period. A scenario for a play was created, and scenes were written, but the group eventually decided that there was not enough interest at that time to justify continuing the group.

Contact was made with other organisations in the area including the Southside Youth Club, where three of the youth workers who had been involved in the community plays wanted to develop theatre with the young members. Over a four-month period, ACTA workers helped to devise and produce a series of youth drama events, with SWOOT members providing lighting and design, using skills learnt during the design courses.

Although the work in South Bath had less effect in the final year than was originally planned, the impact of the work overall was wider than initially envisaged. Following the ACTA model in terms of the third year as a series of skills training courses was not appropriate here. The reasons were various:

- a level of skills training had already been achieved through the previous two community plays and the concurrent design courses
- the gap between the end of *Hot Water* and the start of the skills training schemes was significant
- some participants moved on from the community play into other ventures, including jobs and new drama groups
- other participants started their own initiatives for drama in the community

People attending the skills training course found it hard to be developing a script for a project that had no funding for production, and the main interest of the group was to get a new community play to performance. At the same time, ACTA was entering the busiest period of the *Making a Difference* project, working simultaneously in Stoke Gifford and Bournville. In addition, we were hosting *New Moves*, an international festival of theatre by people with learning difficulties; running three women's theatre projects; working on a project with young people with visual impairment; undertaking youth theatre projects on outlying estates in Bristol. Resources were stretched.

However, SWOOT Community Theatre has now gained charitable status and, following a period of inactivity, there are plans for more community arts in the area as part of a Single Regeneration Budget (SRB) project. The Southside Youth Club continues to organise a good deal of drama activity.

"If you'd said at the beginning of the project that there would be young people coming to a drama club on the estate, everyone would have laughed at you. But it's happening. That's the biggest change that's come about. We know theatre isn't something that's only for the centre of Bath: it's for us here, on our estate."

Lin Lewis, Leader in Charge, Southside Youth Club

3 | **Stoke Gifford**

Prior to *Making a Difference*, ACTA had worked in Stoke Gifford on a community play pilot in the form of a reminiscence project. Through this, a Youth Theatre and Stoke Gifford Community Theatre were formed, and a show entitled *Snapshots* performed.

Out of the Shadows

A *Making a Difference* Project Co-ordinator was appointed in September 1996 to work initially for one day a week, increasing to three days a week from April 1997. Her role was to contact local individuals and groups to publicise the project and attract more members to both the Youth Theatre and the devising group, which had begun to meet weekly at the Youth Centre. Groups contacted included: playgroups, parent and toddler groups, schools, churches, a day centre for older people, local writers and history groups, PHAB club, tea dance club, volunteer bureau, women's institute, guides and scouts - to list but a few. There were regular bulletins in the local press and community newspapers.

A questionnaire was enclosed in 4,000 leaflets distributed to libraries, community centres and doctors' surgeries as well as via local groups, asking people to give their ideas on what the play should be about, and in which era it should be set. The leaflet also enclosed a return slip for people to 'sign up' as performers, writers, musicians, publicity helpers, fundraisers, backstage and front of house workers. In those early days, most return slips were from people wishing to be performers and only a few questionnaires were returned, mostly from people already involved through the devising group or the Youth Theatre. This wasn't surprising. We were working in a place where people didn't have the faintest idea what we were on about. We needed to do much more explaining and persuading before they lost enough of their prejudice about theatre and started to gain confidence in themselves to believe they could make some sort of contribution to the project.

A public meeting in January 1997 brought more local people on board and I spent much time in the area, researching its history and talking to local contacts established through the Co-ordinator.

From September 1996, both the Youth Theatre and devising group worked with Holly Thomas, ACTA's apprentice director, and me every week. Several hundred further questionnaires were circulated asking people for stories about local events or characters, likes and dislikes about the area, how long their family had lived in the area, what message the play should have. Around 50 were returned. The questions also formed the basis of a number of interviews with local individuals and community groups, undertaken by the Co-ordinator and me, as researcher/devisor. In all, around 200 individuals were consulted.

Local people, and in particular the devising groups, put forward many ideas about stories to be included in the show. Two stories that became crucial to the formation of the whole play came from the same devising session. One group member gave his vivid recollections of Hortham Colony, a local institution where he had spent much of his life because he had learning difficulties. A woman spoke of being 'put away' in the early 1930s for having an illegitimate baby. The other group members were deeply moved by these memories, and the central theme of care in the community was chosen. Another of the main issues that emerged was the concern over the vast programme of building in recent years and the lack of local community facilities. New housing developments and office complexes were swallowing up what had previously been green areas.

People began to turn up to devising sessions with poems, songs and ideas for new scenes and even whole scenes written. Gradually the scenario was developed, and, once the devising was completed, it was my task to pull everything together and give structure to all the hard work that had gone on. New ideas continued to surface during the devising process that I incorporated into the play. One such strand was the 'rivalry' between the older established community of Little Stoke and the new area of Bradley Stoke. Local historians living in the area were very helpful, as were local residents in possession of historical documents such as early parish records and photographs. Participants were fascinated by the interesting details being discovered about their area's past.

Whilst the devising was taking place, we made arrangements with Filton High School, the venue for the production, and approached freelancers to work with interested community members and the cast to design the set, lighting and costumes. The school hall was a very large and flexible area and, following discussions with the set and lighting designer, we agreed to put the main action of the performance in the middle of the hall, with the audience on either side. This meant that cast members who were disabled or had mobility problems had no access problems.

The Steering Committee agreed the final version of the script at Easter 1997, copies were printed and the cast list was drawn up. We held a Script Pick-up evening in April at which rehearsal schedules and scripts were given out.

ACTA was able to provide a third director, Lizzie Minnion, and rehearsals began the week after Easter. There was some cast 'drop out', as we expected from our previous experience of community plays, but only a small number. Some found three-hour rehearsals too long, and a few young people found the commitment of rehearsals too much to square with homework. When we had some Saturday and Sunday rehearsals there were a few complaints about clashes with cricket matches, and there was a slight drop in attendance on particularly sunny days in May and June. But by and large the commitment to rehearsals was good. The cast gained in confidence in their performances, always contributing suggestions and ideas about how the play should be interpreted. Some people who had previously joined the group because they wanted to help backstage found that they wanted to take a part.

We recruited volunteers to work with Alan May, the set designer, who built and painted the set and props. After much searching, we found some local storage, although it was not ideal. Storing costumes was even more difficult and costume designer Vania Mills' car began to resemble a mobile wardrobe. In the end, the local scout group kindly allowed us the use of their H.Q. Vania collected and made a huge array of costumes, ably assisted by a small but dedicated band of volunteers. She spoke at length to cast members about what they felt that their characters should wear.

There was not enough money in the budget to appoint either a Production Manager or a Stage Manager, so the Directors took on the former role together with the Co-ordinator, and three ACTA volunteers agreed to share the tasks needed for stage management. Another ACTA volunteer came to rehearsals to work with the younger members of the Youth Theatre. Backstage and front of house helpers distributed 10,000 leaflets and 200 posters. Families and friends were persuaded to buy vast numbers of raffle tickets.

Since the venue was a school, we were not able to start moving in and setting up until less than a week before the first performance. This created a few problems on the technical side, and the cast felt that they needed an extra dress rehearsal in the venue. They were delighted when a television crew from the local BBC news 'Points West' then turned up to film them.

After the first performance of *Out of the Shadows* it became apparent that the audience had gone away and spread the word about how good the show was. For two of the subsequent performances, we had to ask people who had turned up at the door to wait, to make sure that we had enough room to seat them.

The comments made to the front of house volunteers by the audiences were very favourable. People had not expected such a high standard of performance from a community group. Many had been moved to tears by the story. Some commented on the strength of the portrayal of characters by the cast. Others talked about the excellent set and special effects, and were pleased at the way in which the audience had been seated, affording as many people as possible a 'good view'.

Out of the Shadows factfile

- 5 performances in July 1997
- 900 in audience
- 20 people in devising group
- 120 actors and dancers, aged 6 to 94
- 21 musicians
- 50 people involved in design and build of set, making costumes, backstage and front of house

We circulated a questionnaire to all participants either during or at the end of the project and 65 were returned. Here's a selection of responses:

Most enjoyable

"Seeing the young people becoming friends with the retired people in our community."

"Being involved in all aspects of the show."

"Meeting and making new friends that I didn't know existed in my own community."

"The most satisfying thing was to know that it was the people who were in the play that wrote it."

Personal gain

"We have found out about the history of Little Stoke."

"Working with different people especially those with learning difficulties."

"A lot more confidence and a sense of pride."

"It has brought my family a lot closer as several of us acted or helped out."

"Sense of achievement - working in a team, the fun of being with lots of people all sharing the same experience."

"I feel more involved in the community."

"I feel that I have been treated like an equal member of the community."

"It was good to do something rather than hang around or watch TV."

The project had been hard work but great fun. People with very different life experiences and abilities had worked together to make it a success. Our targeting of those who had little or no experience of arts activity had been successful. The important thing for many people was that the project offered a free and local opportunity, and the lack of auditions for performers was a key factor in their involvement.

Many participants came to the group with the idea that they would be 'told' what to do. They found it a new and invigorating experience to discover their own creative and expressive talents. Several spoke of the need they had to find a focus for their lives, which was provided by their involvement with the project. Many others had joined to act but found that their interest extended to learning about direction, costume design and making, fundraising, publicity and so on.

The project had helped to give a positive identity to the area as one where a range of community members could work together to produce a highly moving and professional piece of work. As an area with its share of social problems and scarce resources, the project had gone a long way to raise the morale and counter the apathy of the local community.

Despite the tremendous time commitment on themselves and their families that the production had needed, the cast had an overwhelming desire to carry on after the end of *Out of the Shadows*. Over 70 people attended a meeting in September 1997 to determine the future of the project, and decided to carry on with the following projects:

- the continuation of the very successful youth theatre
- training by ACTA in various theatre skills

- a second community play, for which the Steering Group, with assistance from ACTA, raised funding from local authority departments and the National Lottery Arts for Everyone Express scheme

Ticket to Nowhere

The devising period for this second community play ran from September 1997 to April 1998, during which time the play was created from scratch, scripted and rehearsed. The play involved over 120 people of all ages and abilities from different parts of the five Stoke areas. The training element as set out in our initial *Making a Difference* project plan was extremely successful in this project, with local people shadowing the Director, learning basic devising and writing skills. A training programme in set design, lighting and costume design was set up (funded by Community Education) to run alongside the production, with local people creating designs for the play whilst learning skills for future work. The music and songs for the show were written and scored by two local people, and the musical director volunteered their services. Fundraising for the project was undertaken by the Committee (with the help of their Co-ordinator and ACTA), and box office and front of house were organised by a small group of volunteers.

The show itself was a fantasy, based on the true story of a local area called Nowhere. This was the starting point for a trainload of various characters to embark upon a journey through a series of fantastical situations, during the course of which they discovered the truth about themselves and their fellow passengers. The play was a great success, and named as one of the year's top five theatre shows of 1998 in the regional listings Venue magazine.

Since *Ticket to Nowhere*, Stoke Gifford Community Theatre have continued to meet and work on a variety of projects. The Youth Theatre has been taken over by a participant from the two community plays, who has worked with the young people of the area to devise, write and produce a pantomime, *Cinderemma*. This was produced in February 1999, with 30 young people taking part. Local people who had taken part in the training programme set up during *Ticket to Nowhere* provided music, set and lighting.

Devising sessions for the next community play started in September 1998, facilitated by me, with 18 group members. These sessions focused on creating a script using comedy, rather than local issues, as its starting point. The group worked through sessions on characterisation, plot creation and development, play structure, dialogue, writing from improvisation and writing of lyrics. The play was completed in May 1999, but to date has yet to be produced.

The group is undertaking fundraising for resources to stage this next show. Through a series of planning meetings held with me the group have identified their needs:

- a part-time Co-ordinator 2 days a week
- running costs for an office
- charitable status
- training in management of staff and projects
- training in fundraising

The group has recently changed its name to The Stokes Community Theatre, has created a constitution and is eager to seek charitable status. Its aims are to develop community theatre in the area:

'to promote, maintain, improve and advance education among persons in the Stoke Gifford area by the production of educational plays and the encouragement of the arts.'

'to advance the education of persons in the said area by the provision of workshops and training facilities in the creative and interpretative arts.'

So far over 300 people in the area have been involved in *Making a Difference* and related projects and there is a great deal of local enthusiasm for the initiative to continue. By the end of the project the group was still, however, at a fragile stage of existence and aware of its vulnerability, due in the main to lack of time and professional expertise in co-ordination and fundraising.

4 | **Bournville**

The *Making a Difference* project began in Bournville in April 1996. We faced a very specific group of challenges:

- **apathy:** there was little history of people getting involved in community activity.

- **mistrust:** Bournville is very much a closed community, with a split between older families who have been there since the 1930s, some of which are in the fourth generation, and 'incomers'. A succession of mainly council-led schemes had promised great improvements, but failed to deliver. People were suspicious and cynical about the potential of new schemes.

- **lack of self-confidence:** people had a low estimation of what they could achieve in life and a lack of confidence in themselves and in the area as a whole.

- **low self-esteem:** this lack of confidence led to low self-esteem, both in individuals and in the area as a whole.

Local people had little motivation to get involved in any project that aimed to make things happen on the estate. They basically did not believe that it was possible, and, if it wasn't possible, then why bother? It wasn't worth getting involved because nothing would happen and then any effort they put into it would be wasted. There was also a deep feeling of not wanting to fail at something else or to be set up for ridicule within the community. It was easier to keep out of it, say it couldn't happen, keep safe.

This was a difficult set of circumstances from which to start, so we decided, following discussions with local workers, to take some time to overcome people's suspicions, convince them of the potential of the community play project and get them involved. In the first year of our work we decided just to try to get to know the area, let people get to know us and forge relationships with key players and stakeholders on the estate.

During the first few months, we made links with the Locality Centre[9] staff and its projects including a literacy group and a sewing group, the youth centre staff, a playgroup, headteachers at both primary schools, volunteers at the community centre, a homelessness project, the vicar and William Knowles Resource and Activity Centre for people with learning difficulties. These preliminary meetings were designed to sow the seed.

In May there was an article about the play on the front page of the *Bournville Broadcaster* (a newsletter set up by the Locality Centre as a platform for local organisations) advertising a public meeting which attracted 17 local people and workers. This seemed to us to be quite a low turnout, but workers were vastly encouraged that there was anyone there at all. A Steering Committee was formed to manage the play project in partnership with ACTA comprising residents, the local community worker and the vicar. It met monthly throughout the project and was an essential link between ACTA and the community. Several members of the Steering

---

9 A health and community centre co-funded by the local Health Authority and Social Services

Committee went on to join the devising group and perform in the play.

In September we began a weekly research and writing session at the Locality Centre. This group began very slowly, with three members, but over the course of the autumn interviewed and reached about 20 local people. We had meetings with local organisations and people who were unable or disinclined to attend the research group and circulated several hundred questionnaires to get ideas about the theme and content of the show. Only 30 were returned. This underlined the low level of involvement in this early stage of the project and indicated the reluctance of local people to commit themselves in writing. As time went on, many more people gave answers to our questions through interviews, meetings and informal chats. From this period of research and contact, the following themes and issues arose:

- most people were not born on the estate
- there was a large number of people who had left the estate but then returned, homesick
- most people thought the play should deal with present day issues as well as *"the struggles of the past"*
- issues of concern were: drugs and crime, dirty needles on the street, the area's bad image in the press, need for more facilities, especially shops and a café, lack of community spirit
- the message of the play should be the need for community spirit, and to *"accentuate the positive"*

- the extensive bombing during the Second World War was a particularly vivid memory for the older generation

Yer Tis

We were having limited success in involving adults in the project, so we decided to work with the children and through them to inform, interest and involve their parents and extended family. The most trusted method of communication on the estate was the oldest, word of mouth. With this in mind, we made a link with Windwhistle Primary School and in January 1997 began a weekly visit to the school, working within school time with a Year 6 class. The sessions took place in the school hall and included games, drama exercises and improvisation. The response from the children and staff was enthusiastic and in the third week we introduced the idea of creating and performing a small piece of theatre for the rest of the school to see. We used as material for the piece many of the memories and experiences we had collected during our research and also a small book of local memories, Yer Tis.

Over a period of eight weeks the children worked on creating small scenes from the material supplied, inventing characters, dialogue and a linking narrative. The topic fitted neatly into the school curriculum as the class was studying the Second World War period. Soon pupils were being involved by their teachers in extra research, including visits from older people with memories of the time. They greeted us each week with more stories, details and even artefacts which they had gathered. ACTA provided costumes for each child, props and a sound track to the scenes they had created, and on the day of the show at the end of March spent much extra time rehearsing the piece, which was performed to the rest of the school. The teachers used the work to 'tick the boxes' to give evidence of a variety of key curriculum tasks - including research, interviewing and creative work.

Reaction to this small project was enthusiastic and from then on more people began to take an interest in the community play. Many of the children who took part in this pilot project carried on to take part in the devising group and the community play.

In the first quarter of the second year there were various key developments, the first of which was the appointment of John Loosley, the author of *Yer Tis*, as Play Co-ordinator. A play office was established at the Locality Centre, and John began to forge new contacts in the community, find the extra funds needed for the project and to collate and process information.

The research group continued to meet and was joined by new members, some of them contacts of John Loosely who had been involved in the *Yer Tis* book. There was now a fairly stable group who looked more closely at the issues and themes that had already been collected from the community. The group started to experiment with ideas to explore these issues and themes, whilst telling the story of the estate. The group identified that 'prejudice' would form the core theme of the play, particularly focusing on the prejudice shown to Bournville and Bournville people by those in surrounding areas. The idea was to set against this prejudice stories and memories that would show the positive side of the area.

Bouncy Buses and Crazy Caves

The second pilot project was created in partnership with Bournville Junior School to establish an after-school drama club. Over the first few weeks, over 100 children from the school took part in these sessions, before a group of 30 was selected by lottery. This was a difficult approach for us, but we had to take due regard of the school's limits, our staffing resource and the quality of the children's engagement.

Lizzie Minnion, Holly Thomas and I worked with the group. Over a period of ten weeks we devised a short fantasy piece, taking as its inspiration a school trip to Cheddar caves. The process of creation involved improvisation, discussion and quite advanced drama exercises, freeze and shifting focus, ensemble work, mime and movement. No script was produced for the show, which was left as polished improvisation. The children wrote the words to a new song to end the play. The final piece, *Bouncy Buses and Crazy Caves*, complete with costume, set and live music was performed twice at the school, to children, staff and parents.

The reaction of the audience was extraordinary. It was the first time they had seen a devised piece, and the natural quality of the children's performance, unencumbered by script, alive and expressive, delighted them. The staff were amazed at the level of commitment shown by the group members, the creativity of their imagination, the co-operation between performers of different ages and from different classes. They were particularly impressed by the performance of many group members who were usually known for low achievement and bad behaviour. The parents showed great interest in the community play project and several signed up on the spot to get involved in a wide variety of ways. The play was also seen by several Steering Group members, who up to then had taken ACTA's promise of the benefits of theatre mostly on trust. Here at last was a chance for them to see it in action.

Bouncy Buses and Crazy Caves was only one of the strategies employed during this period to interest local people in the community play project. A leaflet explaining the project's aims, giving a timetable of events and details of the regular devising groups set up for the autumn and including a joining form, went to every house on the estate, to every school child, to every shop and meeting place.

ACTA also had a stall at the Bournville Festival, a celebration organised by local people in conjunction with the Locality Centre. We talked about the project and gave out leaflets. Many of the children from the pilot projects renewed contact and a wide cross-section of local people took the opportunity to meet us.

This process of involvement continued throughout the next 12 months, and included public meetings, local media campaigns and memory lunches. These lunches used the arts to deliver the Locality Centre's policy on raising standards of nutrition on the estate. The lunches used nutritious recipes from the 40s and 60s, giving local people the opportunity to have a free, filling and healthy meal whilst contributing their memories and stories to the community play project. For instance, the 40s soup, created from a Lord Woolton recipe, sparked some anecdotes about rationing and the importance of food that became the inspiration for a whole scene.

Shining Through

In September 1997 three weekly groups - the children's drama club, youth theatre and adult remembering and writing group - were established to devise and script the play. Each was involved in developing the initial ideas and stories identified by the original research group.

The adult group involved all of the research group members, plus a large number of new members. There was a core group of ten, with a further 24 being involved sporadically. The group also linked up with the church drama group, who used improvisation to devise some sections of the play. They soon identified three stories that formed the skeleton of the play:

- the resilience of local people during the war years when the area was badly bombed
- a love story set in the 60s

• the despair of a young girl in the present

Each of these stories was based on the real life experiences of group members and each related to the central theme of prejudice. In the wartime story, evacuees and local children clash, a woman is hounded from the area when she becomes pregnant and a local figure of fun becomes a hero in an air raid. In the 60s part, a young woman from the posh side of Weston falls in love with a boy from Bournville and has to overcome the prejudice of her mother. In the present, a teenager is bullied because she lives in Bournville.

The devising group had to put flesh on the bones, to create characters, dialogue, songs and scenes. Group members developed their confidence at a rapid and remarkable rate. *"It's just like a real play"*, one of them said. The group used a mixture of improvisation and communal writing to devise. I took careful notes that were typed into a script each week and read at the start of the next session. The transformation of chat and scribble into printed text was a source of delight and pride to the devising group. One member would do readings with his family, getting them to read in parts and act out, his granddaughters diving under the kitchen table during the air raid scenes. The play was coming alive in people's lives and homes.

As their confidence in themselves as writers grew, group members wrote whole sections of the script at home and brought them in.

"I don't know how I got involved, it took a lot of courage to come in that first time. But I was curious. I've never been able to speak in a group, but I could in the writing group. Couldn't just sit there saying nothing, I had things to say. I can talk to anyone now."

Marie, devising group member

The group worked though the autumn and winter on the script, finally completing devising in February 1998. As writer/facilitator I drew up the first draft for the group and the Steering Committee and then made the changes suggested and presented the final script.

The children's drama group brought together children from Windwhistle and Bournville Primary Schools, a feat in itself, as rivalries were rife on the estate. Group membership was 50 overall, but there was a core group of 30 who attended throughout. Ages ranged from 5 to 12, which did present some problems from time to time, although in the main the older children were quite happy to work with and help the younger ones. This group was also involved in the devising process, taking certain sections of the play as their own. Over a number of weeks they developed individual characters with histories and personalities and created a large number of scenes. A great deal of their improvisation was incorporated into the script and other sections left to be devised and performed unscripted in each performance.

The youth theatre was not a great success. Designed for the 12-16 age group, the sessions were held in the evening at the local youth centre. Only a handful of young people attended the group, none of whom was involved in the play. The reasons for this lack of success were:

- **venue:** the youth club was just emerging from a difficult time. It had been without a leader for some time, closed for refurbishment and membership had fallen away. When the club did re-open, there was a dispute between the members and the staff which resulted in young people boycotting the club. In addition, the youth club had a bad reputation on the estate, so many young people were too apprehensive or not allowed to attend.

- **timing:** the sessions were at a prime teenage television viewing time.

- **image:** theatre wasn't viewed as something to get involved in.

It was only following outreach sessions at local secondary schools that eventually a large number of young people did get involved in the play.

By the time the play was complete, the various strategies for finding participants had proved very successful. The play had been written for over 100 characters, including 30 children, but with over 50 children wanting to take part, massive rewrites had to take place at the last minute to increase the number of children's speaking parts. This took the cast up to 120 speaking parts. There was a significant number of participants who wanted to be in the show but not speak, and also a number who were interested in dance, so they devised, rehearsed and performed sections of physical theatre within the play.

All participants were cast and invited to the Script Pick-up Night held at the Locality Centre. Until this point we were still quite unsure about what the turnout would be, but our worries were unfounded. The Locality Centre was awash with people that evening, all in a high state of excitement, eager to see the play, find out their part and look up their scenes. Nearly three-quarters of the cast turned up and John Loosley contacted those who couldn't make it to arrange an alternative pick-up.

Rehearsals started in late March and continued for twelve weeks bringing together the different sections of the community, working with a joint focus. Many of the adults had not worked with children and young people before and this did cause the occasional difficulty. In the main, however, there was little tension and the integration of people with and without learning difficulties for the first time on the estate was a particular success. People quickly found mutual respect through working together, sharing laughs, appreciating each other's performances.

Friendships formed that lasted beyond the rehearsal room and beyond the end of the community play.

> *"I've been really impressed with the talents and ideas of the cast and their level of commitment. Atmospheres during rehearsals have been brilliant, and the cast have given us great ideas for the direction of the piece."*
>
> Lizzie Minnion, Co-Director, *Shining Through*

As rehearsals progressed, the cast members were increasingly impressed at what they were achieving together, scenes often earning spontaneous applause from those watching. This was a tremendous boost to the confidence of those performing, especially those for whom it was their first experience.

During March to May, music, front of house, design and costume, lighting and sound tapes were organised. A series of production meetings was held, involving the ACTA team, freelancers and Co-ordinator. Design and making sessions were run in the community and a small group of local musicians gathered to rehearse the seven songs and the incidental music for the show. A backstage team was recruited from local people, and many others for the front of house. Tickets were printed and sold from the Locality Centre. The staff were surprised at the interest in the show, complaining good-humouredly that they weren't getting time to do anything but sell tickets.

A regular flow of press releases to local press, radio and television ensured that the profile of the project was high, although it proved impossible to draw the local television cameras down from Bristol. A poster and leaflet campaign all through Weston-Super-Mare targeted holidaymakers as well as locals, and in the last weeks of the rehearsal period, cast members walked the sea-front in costume, handing out leaflets.

Shining Through was performed at Wyvern School at the end of May 1998.

"The value of the play should not be underestimated. It has brought together age groups who may not normally meet, and has helped to change a few opinions; allowed individuals to shine; and given the whole community an opportunity to display the positive side of living on the Bournville estate. There is now a stronger sense of community pride. But above all it has provided those involved with a great deal of fun."

Claire Novak, Community Health Worker,
Bournville Locality Centre

Shining Through factfile

- 5 performances in May 1998
- 1000 in the audience
- 80 people involved in research and devising
- 110 cast members
- 6 musicians
- 29 crew
- 18 front of house

Front of house staff remarked on the reminiscing going on amongst the audience during the interval. Cast members commented on how surprised their families and friends were at their performances.

"I shall have to change the way I think about the Bournville from now."

"I didn't think it would be so professional."

"It's brought back so many memories."

"I didn't know that my children were so talented."

The whole estate was alive with the play. After the first night the other performances either sold out or exceeded 90% capacity. As the performance week continued the growth of interest on the estate escalated. The cast became captivated by the experience. Many people popped into the venue during the day, helping to clear up from the previous night, ironing and getting costumes ready, arranging to re-rehearse scenes that had gone wrong the previous night, or just to be there.

The effect of the play went wider than the estate, with good press coverage ensuring that the whole of Weston knew that it was taking place. An estimated 20% of the audience came from outside the estate. This was seen as a real measure of success, as non-residents rarely venture on to the Bournville estate. Participants reported overhearing conversations about the play in pubs and shops all over the town and outlying villages, with people who had seen it urging others not to miss out.

The final two performances of the play earned standing ovations from the audience, a spontaneous expression of affirmation that left all cast members elated. The main topic of conversation at the impromptu party that followed the last night was, *"What next? When do we do the next play?"*

Ten days after the end of the performance week, ACTA organised and facilitated an informal evaluation evening. This included a chance to watch a video of the show, to sign up for other projects and to discuss the play and ideas for the future. Over 90 people attended, showing great enthusiasm for what they had been involved with and for future projects.

"Shining Through was a runaway success with all five performances virtually a sell-out. It attracted a lot of attention from beyond the estate, and visitors were heard to say afterwards that they would have to re-assess their views on the Bournville and its people. Within the estate it has fostered greater understanding and mutual respect between the different lifestyles and needs of the groups that make up the community. An example of this was the support given by children in the cast, some from difficult backgrounds, to an elderly lady who had injured her leg. This support was given instinctively and unrequested and would not, I feel, have happened previously."

Clare Herford, Community Social Worker, Bournville estate

Bournville Community Arts

During the run-up to the community play, ACTA workers had begun discussing with the Steering Group the need for follow-up projects. In other areas we had seen the enthusiasm created by a community play frustrated by lack of funds immediately afterwards. We felt it was important with Bournville, as with Stoke Gifford, that some projects were set up to provide continuing opportunities for local people. The Steering

Group decided to give itself an identity beyond its original role and, in early 1998, became Bournville Community Arts (BCA) with its own constitution and policy, and began the process of gaining charitable status.

During planning meetings facilitated by ACTA workers, the members of BCA felt that they wanted to promote a broad range of community arts activities that included, but was not exclusively, theatre. These included a community music project, a dance/fitness programme, fine and public art, a range of learning activities around the arts, and arts activities for children and young people. BCA were granted funding by North Somerset Council for the continuation of the Co-ordinator's post after the community play, and were also funded by Children in Need for the continuation of the children's drama club.

In our initial project proposal this period of the *Making a Difference* project was to be concerned with a second community production, with training opportunities for local people to learn skills needed to create their own projects. Experience in Southmead had shown that formal training courses were not appropriate in these situations, and that learning had its best outcomes when carried out informally through practically working towards an end project. With this in mind, and considering BCA's desire to develop projects wider than theatre, ACTA proposed the creation of an outdoor community celebration for the weekend before Christmas.

The X-mas Files

In September 1998, ACTA began sessions again on the Bournville estate, with the children's drama club for 6 to 12 year olds, and a devising group for all other ages. The two groups met back-to-back on Tuesday evenings and were very popular, with over 30 children at the early session, and a group of 22 at the later session, including older people, adults, teenagers and people with learning difficulties. This second group reduced in number to 15 after the first five sessions, with several of the adults, having wanted to work on another play, not being interested in the idea of an outdoor performance.

Alan May, ACTA's designer, had wide experience of outdoor projects, including carnival, street theatre and pyrotechnics. He and I co-led the sessions which blended different artforms, including visual arts, lantern making, clay modelling, mask making, costume, as well as drama, devising, creative writing and theatre games and exercises.

Both groups created ideas during the first sessions, working around the Christmas theme. A basic story was agreed: a group of alien school children land on earth on a field trip to collect facts about human behaviour and the phenomenon of Christmas. Over the next eight weeks each group created a series of scenes being disrupted by aliens trying to discover the meaning of Christmas. The children's group also designed and made lanterns for the procession and created alien masks. Design sessions were held weekly, two at Windwhistle School and a Saturday workshop at St Andrew's Church. The programme for the evening was drawn up:

- a piece of street theatre, to get attention
- a procession, to gather an audience and entertain people in their houses
- a theatre performance in the church
- a fireworks display
- food and drink

The performance began with carol singers astonished by explosions in the street and aliens landing; then a brass band led a procession of aliens, giant puppets and performers in costume around the streets of the estate, lit by lanterns. The effect was immediate. People flocked out of their houses to see the procession: many of them joined on, following the procession to the church. As the audience approached the church, a giant knife and fork chasing a giant turkey entertained them. Over 250 people of all ages packed into the church to watch the performance and stayed to enjoy the fireworks and food afterwards.

The whole evening exceeded everyone's expectations in a range of ways:

- **access:** the procession made everyone aware of the event. People who could not join in because of mobility difficulties were still able to enjoy part of it from their doorstep. The whole event was free and so accessible to people on low incomes. The free food in particular was a great success and the only hot meal of the day for many families.

- **audience:** the event took place at the heart of the estate so the whole audience was made up of local residents, many of whom had not seen *Shining Through*, which had been performed at a venue on the edge of the estate.

- **sense of occasion:** the event captured the imagination and curiosity of local people: strange and exciting things were happening in everyday locations!

- **celebration:** the sharing of the fireworks and food, as well as the performance, gave the whole event an air of community celebration.

- **validation:** many people commented on how amazed they were that such a huge event was taking place on their estate. The 20 minutes of professional pyrotechnics were an important part of this: many classed it as the best display they had ever seen. The whole of the estate must have seen the display bursting over their streets and houses. For the rest of Weston, the spectacle of positive celebration in the skies above Bournville had never been seen before. There was a feeling of *"We must be worth something; this must be a good place to be if this sort of thing happens here."*

In all, over 100 people were involved in *The X-mas Files* event, as makers, performers, helpers and musicians, an audience of 250 saw the performances, and hundreds, if not thousands, saw the procession and fireworks.

In January 1999 activities continued on the Bournville estate in the form of a children's drama group, a youth theatre and an adult group. All three groups were successful in attracting large numbers of members, in excess of 20 in the children's group, a staggering 23 in the youth theatre, and 14 adults. Each group began working on devising and creating their own individual show, wanting some time with their own peer group following the two joint projects. There was a degree of training going on in all three groups, but particularly with the adult group, where the whole process of play-making through characterisation, plotting, structuring, devising to writing was carefully undergone by the whole group, with several members taking responsibility for writing, and several others for directing. Key members of the community learned a range of skills, which proved essential to the development of future projects. The resulting play, *Death on the Pier*, was directed and produced by the group to a huge audience from the estate.

The Bournville part of the *Making a Difference* programme seemed, at the end of the three years of the project, to have great potential for the future. The factors for this were various:

timescale: the project was timed well, the long lead-up period proving essential in getting local people to a stage where they could trust the project and get involved.

partnerships: the project had strong and committed partners in the area: the community workers, church, primary schools, and particularly the Locality Centre. The potential of the arts project as a means of individual and social regeneration was recognised by many from the outset, and their support was vital.

location: Bournville is a community isolated from the rest of the town, cut-off by railway lines, with no through route. It is well-defined geographically and socially and, although people were lacking in confidence, there was a sense of identity, albeit often expressed in negative terms.

attitudes: the area had no previous experience of community arts projects and, once the initial suspicion had been dispelled, the participants were enthused by the excitement of the project and their own potential. There is now a solid history of successful community arts which will inform the future.

"When I came to the Bournville estate in 1994, it was an area without hope. This was all there was to life, you lived on a round of benefits, trying to make ends meet, never having a job, never having any prospects of a job, that's how people really felt. But what's happened is that there is a range of things that are now available on their doorstep for which they need no qualification. They can just walk in off the street and join in. And that's made the change, the whole atmosphere of the estate has changed, and a large part of that process has been due to the community play, and the work of ACTA over the last three years."

Claire Novak, Community Health Worker,
Bournville Locality Centre

turning points   MAKING A DIFFERENCE

How our aims were met across the project as a whole and the **successes and learning points**

SUCCESSES AND LEARNING

Following my descriptions of the individual projects that comprised *Making a Difference*, I want to look at how our aims were met across the project as a whole and to consider the learning points.

Our aim of involving people who do not normally get involved in community activities was addressed through a programme of targeting these excluded groups. As well as reaching single parents and their children, older people, people with learning difficulties and unemployed people we reached others, in particular people with mental health needs, young people and families on low incomes.

People with learning difficulties were involved in each project, with particular success in the Stoke Gifford and Bournville projects where they have continued an involvement with further projects beyond *Making a Difference*. Single parents were encouraged to get involved by creating characters for them and their children in the play, so that the whole family could take part. In some cases, however, particularly for parents with very small children, the lack of funds for a créche or childcare costs meant that some enthusiastic participants had to drop out of the play after a while. This oversight in funding is certainly one we shall address in future projects.

The majority of adult performers in all shows were unemployed, whether through retirement, lack of opportunity to work, caring commitments or disability. Very few unemployed men of working age were involved in the projects. This reflected low numbers of men involved overall (only 20% participants were male), and this lack of engagement was experienced in other initiatives in these areas.

"It is impossible to involve young men from this estate in anything. It goes against the macho image to be seen to care about anything ... it's not only ACTA that has problems involving the young men ... all local projects have the same problem."

Clare Novak, Community Health Worker,
Bournville Locality Centre

There is a difficult choice here: whether to arrange future projects to attract young men at the expense of other members of the community with identified needs, or to accept their non-involvement. Women, in particular, have benefited hugely from the projects - growing in confidence, making new career and educational choices. For instance, one woman who in 1997 had to muster all her courage to come to her first writing session on the Bournville estate, stayed with the project, joined the Bournville Community Arts Committee and became a local Councillor in 2000.

Approximately 40% of participants in the project were between the ages of 5 to 20, with the majority of them aged 6 to 15. It is hard to over-emphasise the importance of engaging young people in creative and positive activity. In all four areas there was a perceived lack of communication between young people and other sections of the community. The project made great improvements to the level of communication and understanding between different ages.

"The most enjoyable part of Out of the Shadows has been seeing the young people and teenagers becoming friends and on first name terms with the retired people in our community."

Anne Ball, Little Stoke

"I see, in the long run, that the children who are involved in this will be much more able to get involved in the decision-making processes about what happens on the estate, because they will have the confidence to speak up for themselves."

**Clare Novak, Community Health Worker,
Bournville Locality Centre**

Each of the four areas has produced a youth theatre group, recognised as fulfilling an important function in the rest of the community. Youth workers have also incorporated theatre practice into their clubs.

"Drama has become a part of everything we do in the club now, and the young people are really up for it. Not only do we have a regular youth theatre group, but also every time we look at an issue, like drugs or something, we use drama and role-play as a way of exploring the issues. We would never have done that before the project. That's been the biggest impact on this community."

Lynne Lewis, Southside Youth Club

We wanted to ensure the work created by participants addressed local issues. The process of consultation and devising by local people resulted in themes that reflected people's sense of their particular community as well as those that arose out of the experiences of individuals within the community. *Ticket to Nowhere* and *The X-mas Files* were interesting in that both, as second productions, took a more fantastical theme, but still had local issues at their heart. *Ticket to Nowhere* dealt with the importance of people working together and tolerance between different sections of the community. *The X-mas Files* dealt with issues of understanding between different cultures and took a hard look at human behaviour.

We also aimed to foster a sense of community spirit by providing a voice for local concerns. One of participants' most regular comments is about community spirit: making new friends with people they wouldn't usually have contact with, feeling part of the community and having a greater understanding of its past.

"The sense of community was brilliant - all working together. I felt very proud to play someone who lived through all those times on the Bournville."

Heather Puddick, participant, *Shining Through*

It is probably as much the experience of working together that fosters this sense of community spirit, as the opportunity to voice local concerns.

"Stoke Gifford Community Theatre created something quite special with this giant, vigorous production, which drew together so many local people and glued them together with an obvious sense of pleasure and achievement; the spirit of this community is very much alive."

Venue magazine review of *Out of the Shadows*, July 1997

The subject matter of the play is of the utmost importance: having a play about their own area, about their own lives, gives a value to the participants.

"My daughter came to me in tears and said, 'That's the first time I've ever been proud of coming from Southmead.'"

Participant, *Lifelines*

The arts events had the effect of making people feel better about where they live, having seen positive things happening around them.

"So far the project has made a real impact in tackling the causes of poverty through their programme of Community Arts. ACTA have given people the chance to discover their creativity and make links with others, thereby improving their feelings of self-confidence and raising the self-esteem of the estate by making it a better place to live."

Claire Herford, Community Social Worker, Bournville estate

We also intended to make the work a focus for discussion and draw wide attention to the positive aspects and potential of people on the estates. The fact that the projects were happening at all provided a first level of discussion in communities where there had been little positive action previously. During the consultation process people talked with each other and discovered many things in common, a shared history and joint concerns.

The next level of discussion was amongst the participants in the devising group, then later the cast. The creation and performance of the script made many people aware for the first time of local history, and their part in it, and brought to the forefront local issues that prompted further interest and discussion.

The third level was during the performance week, where the high profile of the community plays drew attention from local media and people in the surrounding areas. Both *Hot Water* and *Out of the Shadows* were featured on local television and all plays had extensive radio and newspaper coverage alerting people from the surrounding communities to their existence.

Another aim was to challenge negative stereotypes that contribute to a sense of disempowerment. We had to address participants' views of themselves as individuals, participants' (and audiences') views of people from different sections of the community and the views of people outside towards those living in the area.

The effect on participants' view of themselves was overwhelmingly positive. During the rehearsals for *Out of the Shadows*, the majority of people said the most significant change for them was *"being better at acting, and making new friends"* and by the end of the show, 80% of the same group noted the major change as a growth in self-confidence.

"I always thought that in order to write you needed a university education or an exciting and varied life."

Participant, *Making a Difference*

"As a result of taking part in the devising group I gained more confidence to speak to people, so I have now enrolled in three courses at the college - numeracy, communication skills and basic computer skills."

Participant, *Shining Through*

"As a worker in the community I see the positive change/increased confidence in local people who took part in the project. In some cases it was the reason they kept living."

Penny McKissock, Co-ordinator, Southside Health Project

In terms of people's attitudes to others, the shared focus of the play gave people the opportunity to meet with a cross-section of the community, and an incentive to get on with them.

"There was a great satisfaction from being involved with so many different age groups (being 70 myself), also working with disabled people - they were great."

Participant, *Out of the Shadows*

"I now have a different view of people with learning difficulties."

Participant, *Hot Water*

"I think it made us all tolerant to our fellow citizens, and realise that we are a complex mixture of personalities and needs."

Participant, *Out of the Shadows*

The themes of the plays, in particular in the Bournville project, challenged the negative stereotypes held by the wider community living around the four areas.

> *"On several occasions I was stopped in the High Street and congratulated on my performance. These were people I'd never met before."*

Participant, *Shining Through*

The creation of a visible project, managed by the participants themselves, helped break the cycle of negativity, sense of disempowerment and marginalised social activity created by living in the area.

Our final aim was to develop people's skills to enable them to manage community theatre projects independently from ACTA. Each group received training appropriate to its needs and used this to develop and manage independent projects after *Making a Difference,* but only Stoke Gifford and Bournville actually set up independent community theatre groups.

In Southmead and South Bath, it proved difficult to maintain the momentum of the community groups set up following the community play projects. In Southmead *Making a Difference* had only one year to run, and although there was a great deal of interest from local people in leading their own community theatre projects, there was not the degree of expertise needed within the community to continue without the help of facilitators. In South Bath, the Co-ordinator of *Hot Water* left immediately following the play that created a continuity gap and we weren't able to provide all the support that SWOOT Community

Theatre needed. Newly empowered participants moved on to new interests, new places. One young woman with moderate learning difficulties gained the confidence to leave her parental home and become independent. Many people went on to join other drama groups; many of the young people became involved in drama projects at the local youth club. In this sense the 'failure' to establish a fully functioning independent community theatre group should not actually be seen as such.

From Stoke Gifford and Bournville we learnt that, no matter how successful the projects were, the third year of formal training courses and passing on of skills to local people to lead their own group, was not, on reflection, an achievable aim. It takes longer to pass on all the skills necessary for groups to become stable enough to exist completely without support. It also takes time for an area to come to terms with the radical changes in self-image engendered by the process. The project produced vital and effective groups of local people energised and empowered to want to carry on, but needing a longer period of support to fulfil their potential. *Making a Difference* just began the process of empowerment in areas of social exclusion, and ACTA have made it a priority to seek ways to ensure support for these important fledgling groups.

The Turning Points

questionnaire was sent to over 500 people ranging from those involved in recent projects, to those who participated in the 1980s.

TURNING POINTS

It was my frustration with the difficulty of providing evidence of the impact of participation in the arts that led me to explore models of evaluation and measurement. As often with these situations, you set off with the sense of a lone explorer trying to beat a difficult path through tangled undergrowth, only to find that not only have others been there before you, but also that they have built a motorway. Many organisations have been involved in such research, including Comedia, the Joseph Rowntree Foundation and the Government's Policy Action Team.[10]

102–103

The reasons for the sudden interest in developing this research include, I suggest: the age and tenacity of the community arts movement; the change of government in 1997 and the subsequent changes in policy; the use of arts in regeneration projects over the last ten years forcing arts practitioners to evaluate their work; the arts identified as a 'good cause' in the National Lottery.

Many funding bodies have responded to the new place of participatory arts within the mainstream in their policies. So it would be easy to think that there is no longer a case to be made, or rather that the case had been so widely accepted that further work is unnecessary. But there is still a long way to go and many more to convince. There is also a

10 Matarrasso, F. *Use or Ornament? The Social Impact of Participation in the Arts* (Stroud: Comedia, 1997); Wolheim, B. *Culture makes Communities* (York: Joseph Rowntree Foundation, 1998) and Policy Action Team 10 *A Report to the Social Exclusion Unit: Arts & Sport* (London: Department of Culture, Media and Sport, 1999)

place in any canon of knowledge for a little more, for different angles, to add weight to the argument. From ACTA's point of view, I wanted to consider the *Making a Difference* project within the context of our work over the last fifteen years, and in particular to evaluate individuals' own measurement of the impact of community theatre in their lives subsequent to participation.

To research this, I designed the *Turning Points* questionnaire, which was sent to over 500 people ranging from those involved in recent projects, including *Making a Difference*, to those who participated in the 1980s. Some questionnaires had tracked people over several addresses, so the return rate of 13% overall was pleasing and the return rate of 28% from participants in the 1980s surprisingly high. Here are the main results:

What did you do?

	No. of responses	% of total responses
Everything	8	8.0%
Devising and acting	32	29.0%
Acting	44	40.0%
Stage management	2	1.8%
Design	9	8.2%
Writing	4	3.7%
Front of House	4	3.7%
Co-ordination	3	2.8%
Sound and music	3	2.8%

"Everything! It started with acting and went on to cover all aspects of theatre work from devising, to stage design, lighting sound, and stage management. It even involved going on tour, staying up all night and making millions of sandwiches!"

Sarah Gillman, Kids' Theatre, 1985-87

Had you ever been involved in theatre before taking part in the ACTA project? If so, what did you do?

	No. of answers	% of total responses
Never involved before	42	64.6%
At school	10	15.4%
Local dramatics	5	7.6%
Pantomimes	4	6.1%
Girls Friendly Society	1	1.5%
Songtime Theatre Group	1	1.5%
Operatic group	1	1.5%
Did not answer	1	1.5%

104–105

If you had never been involved in theatre before, what stopped you?

	No. of answers	% of total responses
Lack of opportunity	20	31.2%
Lack of confidence/ stage fright	13	20%
Thought theatre was 'elite & cliquey'	2	3.8%
Never thought about it	2	3.8%
Lack of finance	1	1.5%
Didn't realise it could be so enjoyable	1	1.5%
Did not answer	25	38.5%

"I never had access to theatre, it was not part of my family's culture, there was none at school, it was never available. In my house we watched telly and that was pretty much it."

Fleur Darkin, Kingswood Youth Theatre, 1986-89

"The biggest factor had to be financial; I was a child from a one-parent family and we were not in a position to pay for private drama or acting and so on."

What (if anything) do you feel you personally gained from your participation in the project?

92% answered this question and identified a positive gain for themselves. I did not give any suggested answers. Many people felt they had gained in more than one way. The results show a significant incidence of similarity of experience amongst the participants. The positive percentages do not imply negatives: e.g. because 24% of people identified skill development as a personal gain, does not mean that 76% did not gain skills, only that they did not include that in their answer.

		No. of answers	% of total responses
106–107	Confidence	32	54%
	Enjoyment	30	46%
	New friends	20	31%
	Skills development	16	24%
	Community spirit	16	24%
	Social awareness	15	23%
	Sense of achievement	8	12%
	Work	2	3%

"I gained the confidence to carry on and study drama at night school, and now at the fine age of 25 belong to a Bristol operatic society."

"This was such a positive factor in growing up: being involved in the community, experiencing difference. Personally it was important formatively in gaining independence, assertiveness, mixing with self-age groups. The pleasure and satisfaction from completing a project, or rather seeing it through from initial gestation to performance. The balance between direction and creative autonomy was very good so that we felt we were producing our own thing, but wholly with support, guidance and expertise. Because this was part of my childhood, I just see that as integral to my self-development, so there weren't changes afterward so much as choices linked to that experience. Although I went on to do Theatre Studies, drama isn't part of my career, and the gains are more to do with perspectives and pleasures in performing, confidence and even skills and the experience of achieving personal/collective goals from such an early age. The pleasure of such collaboration is something I miss now."

"In general it has made me a lot more outgoing, assertive and creative and has helped me to develop leadership skills and groupwork skills."

Did anything in your life change
as a result of your involvement?
If so, what did you do after the
project you may not have done
before?

	% of total responses
Positive changes	72%
No change	20%
Did not answer	8%

Those who identified positive life changes gave a
range of responses, and again many gave more
than one area of change:

108–109

Personal growth, change of attitudes	34%
Further education and career development	18%
More creative activities, drama, writing	31%
More involved in community	12%

*"So much! We formed our own
community group and developed
projects of our own."*

*"I have had two poems published in
small magazines which I would not
have attempted before."*

"I think the biggest change came in my ideas surrounding my future. When I was younger I dreamed of being an actress or a dancer, but I thought my only real option was to work in a shop. My involvement with ACTA shifted this dream into a reality, and I felt as though acting could be an option. After leaving school I took an extra GCSE in dance, and the following year joined the BTech in Performing Arts at City of Bath College."

"Learned to use the bus."

"I felt that my personal values and aims were better understood by my circle of friends through the project. I became more confident and in control through having to talk to the media. I had held those people in some awe previously."

"It led to a career in theatre that has taken me to work in Manchester, in the West End and at the Sydney Opera House."

"I have gone on to become more involved in local arts organisations and have helped to organise some myself. I have exhibited several of my own pieces of artwork. I have read some of my poetry to groups of people within the community. I also find now that I can communicate with all sorts of people through creative activities and have a much greater understanding of the difficulties that can arise through lack of communication."

"I found work!!!"

How do you rate your experience of participation in community theatre as an important event in your life?

(where 0 = unimportant and 10 = extremely important)

Number on scale	% of responses
8-10	44%
5-7	23%
1-4	28%
did not answer	5%

How often do you think about it ?

(where 0 = never and 10 = all the time)

Number on scale	% of responses
8-10	29%
5-7	51%
1-4	14%
did not answer	6%

What sort of experience was it ?

(where 0 = negative and 10 = positive)

Number on scale	% of responses
8-10	81%
3-7	16%
did not answer	3%

How much effect has it had on you?

(where 0 = none and 10 = lots)

Number on scale	% of responses
8-10	71%
3-7	23%
did not answer	6%

When I broke down the statistics by date (i.e. respondents from the 1980s, 1990-95 and 1996-99), a large number of participants from the 1980s rated their involvement highest on the above scale. Many of these respondents were involved in ACTA's early youth theatre work as teenagers and are now young adults. Nearly all of them acknowledge the great importance of their participation in:

- the development of their personalities and attitudes
- educational choices and development
- career choice and development
- important life friendships

The factors for this perception of impact may be:

- distance from the experience makes it possible to view it in full perspective
- a greater length of time within which the impact can take effect
- nostalgia for youth
- that involvement when participants were in formative years meant that the potential for impact was greater

112–113

"Community theatre is a really positive technique for introducing people to new ideas - perhaps it is particularly important for kids and teenagers, because it helps to break stereotypes and overcome prejudice - before kids turn into adults that are 'set in their ways'."

Sarah Gillman, participant 1985-87

These participants from the 1980s were glad of the opportunity to put on paper what they saw as the great benefits their participation has had on their life.

"It was a very empowering experience. As a teenager when everything was pretty awful, unhappy family, self-confidence non-existent, it was the one light in a bleak experience. ACTA offered me the key to creativity, the key to colour in a monochrome world; the drama workers listened to what we wanted, and felt and meant the world to me. I got to meet people from the other side of town, and realised they weren't superior. It gave me confidence to enter the world of education, and I now have a first class degree and MA with distinction in cultural studies. ACTA sowed a lot of seeds!"

Fleur Darkin

A similar level of positive responses has come from those involved during the last two years, predominantly the *Making a Difference* project. Here the experience is still fresh in the memory of the participants and accordingly they score it high as a positive experience. A smaller proportion, however, rate it high on the effect it has had on them, or on any changes that may have happened in their lives as a result. This could be because:

• it has had little effect on them

• they are too close to the experience to view it in perspective

- not enough time has elapsed within which the impact of their participation can be felt

It would be interesting to return to these same participants in several years' time to see whether their perception of the impact of participation on their lives has changed at all.

Which words describe your involvement?

	Number of responses	% of total respondents
Fun	60	92%
Motivating	52	80%
Energising	41	63%
Important	36	55%
Significant	33	51%
Addictive	25	38%
Empowering	23	35%
Frustrating	7	11%

114–115

None of the negative choices, with the exception of 'Frustrating', was selected by any of the respondents. All respondents viewed their involvement positively, particularly as 'Fun'. The large percentage of respondents identifying the enjoyment they had gained from the experience reminds me, as a worker, how important it is never to lose sight of the 'fun' involved in a project.

What have you done/felt since your involvement with ACTA that you feel is connected to your involvement?

	% of total respondents
Found new friends	68%
More involvement in the arts	43%
More aware of issues	38%
More assertive	37%
Happier	37%
New interests	32%
More involved in community	32%
Gone on to further education	17%
New relationship	12%
New job	8%
Career change	6%

Although the highest percentages are in the areas of social development there is a significant incidence of people who have moved on to further education, new jobs and new relationships through their involvement. In the sample from the 1980s, there was a higher incidence of perceived impact, with 7 of the 14 participants (50%) who returned questionnaires linking their further education to their involvement. There is also a high score for the development of assertiveness linked to involvement.

Is there anything else that's changed that isn't listed?

"I spoke up for myself and always questioned the way things worked."

"Raised awareness of how social and political issues can be addressed through community theatre."

Is there anything thing else at all you'd like to add that's not covered in the questionnaire?

"I really appreciate the skills involved in theatre now and try to go to more professional shows."

"It does people good to be stretched. We all have hidden talents that can be brought out with professional help. The experience must be even more significant for learning disabled people. I now have much more understanding after working on productions with learning disabled."

"I have seen in myself, and in so many different participants, the incredible life changes and the wide range of changes possible from such a simple concept."

The great majority of respondents viewed their participation in ACTA projects as a positive impact on their lives. This participation has, in a large number of cases, significantly changed their lives. This has been either on a personal level, with changed attitudes and new interests; on a social level, with a greater circle of friends and more involvement in the community; or in the areas of education and career development; and in some cases even new relationships. There is some evidence to suggest that the further away from the involvement, the greater is the perception of the impact of that involvement on the participants' lives. There is room here, I feel, for a longer-term study, along the lines of the *7 Up* series of documentaries, where a group of seven individuals have been followed at seven-year intervals since 1963. A similar study, following participants in community arts projects over an extended period of time, has been proposed by ACTA and is being considered by Bristol City Council and South West Arts as a potential project. The interest in evaluation in this form shows no sign of slackening. If the results of the modest survey undertaken for this evaluation are any proof, there is a great deal of work still to do in examining and proving the positive effects of participation in the arts on the lives of individuals.

POSTSCRIPT

Since the body of this book was completed, ACTA have developed work with communities in conjunction with the National Lottery Charities Board (Community Fund) with a project centred on the adjoining Bristol districts of Hengrove and Stockwood. This three-year programme, *Taking Stock, Making Change*, has involved working closely with local people to initiate and co-ordinate a raft of small projects including youth arts, a community garden, local history books, creative writing and a community website. And, of course, community theatre and large-scale community plays. ACTA are at present putting together project plans with two other local areas to develop community play programmes based on the *Making a Difference* model, but with changes that have come from the learning points from the original project.

I continue to receive letters and phone calls from past participants, who have *"just heard"* about this book and want to give their comments and let me know how their lives changed as a result of involvement with